WOULD YOU

RATHER FOR KIDS

Valentine's Day Edition

How to Play

Step 1

Split into two teams whether that be boys vs girls, kids vs parents, or any mix of your choice. If possible, also assign one person as a referee.

Step 2

Decide who gets to go first. Which team can do the most pushups? Which team can guess the number between 1 and 10 from someone not playing the game? Or just some good old fashioned rock paper scissors?

Step 3

The starting team has to ask a question from the book and the opposing team has 10 seconds to not only choose an option but to also give a meaningful reason as to why they chose what they did. The referee decides whether the answer is acceptable.

Step 4

The team can discuss their answer together but only one player can give the answer. The person answering has to alternate every turn.

Step 5

If the player who is answering can't choose or give a good reason then that player is out for the game and can't answer anymore or be involved in the team discussion.

Step 6

Repeat until all players are eliminated.

Would you rather...

Laugh HO HO HO as your usual laugh **OR** *have a squeaky voice like an elf?*

Would you rather...

Be the only person that doesn't get a Valentine's gift **OR** *be the only person that gave one?*

Would you rather...

*Never have to pay for clothes again **OR** food?*

Would you rather...

*Celebrate Valentine's Day on a snowy cold day **OR** a hot sunny day?*

Would you rather...

*Go to Disneyworld **OR** Universal Studios for a 3-day Valentine's Day trip?*

Would you rather...

*Be able to talk with dogs **OR** speak an extra language?*

Would you rather...

*Get cash **OR** presents for Valentine's Day?*

Would you rather...

*Have super vision **OR** super hearing as a super power?*

Would you rather...

Give an offensive Valentine's Day card **OR** *receive one?*

Would you rather...

Spend a day with family **OR** *friends?*

Would you rather...

*Have your heart always beat so loud that everyone could hear it **OR** always have bright red skin?*

Would you rather...

*Be itchy **OR** sticky for a whole day?*

Would you rather...

*Get a lot of Valentines from people that you don't really know **OR** just one from someone special?*

Would you rather...

*Listen to One Direction **OR** the Jonas Brothers?*

Would you rather...

Be able to control the temperature **OR** *be able to fly?*

Would you rather...

Be the host of a Valentine's Day party **OR** *a guest of one?*

Would you rather...

*Go watch a movie **OR** play mini golf as a first date?*

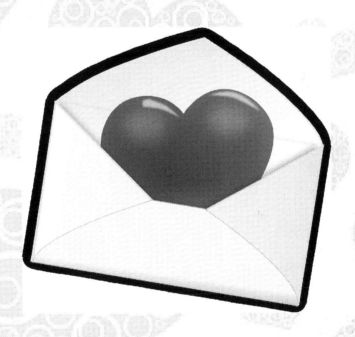

Would you rather...

*Solve global warming **OR** end world hunger?*

Would you rather...

*Have your crush's dad be Rambo **OR** the Terminator?*

Would you rather...

*Give up texting **OR** calling?*

Would you rather...

*Be able to tell if someone is lying **OR** always get away with a lie?*

Would you rather...

*Give up chocolates **OR** candy?*

Would you rather...

*Have an oversized head **OR** a very high pitched voice?*

Would you rather...

*Get a Valentine through email **OR** physical mail?*

Would you rather...

*Get Valentine's Day candy from your teacher **OR** a pass on homework for the day?*

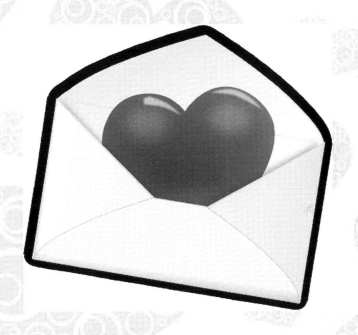

Would you rather...

*Have your breath come out as Darth Vader's **OR** your voice come out as Yoda's?*

Would you rather...

*Go to a boring Valentine's Day party with amazing food **OR** a fun one but with terrible food?*

Would you rather...

*Have the ability to freeze time **OR** travel in time?*

Would you rather...

*Not be able to listen to music **OR** not watch TV?*

Would you rather...

*Attend a Valentine's Day party at school **OR** someone's house?*

Would you rather...

*Find your true love **OR** have your dream job?*

Would you rather...

*Be trapped in a room with 100 spiders for a day **OR** eat 3 spiders?*

Would you rather...

*Be able to eat only red foods **OR** white foods for Valentine's Day?*

Would you rather...

*For 5 minutes, wear a snowsuit in the desert **OR** be naked in Antarctica?*

Would you rather...

*Vacation in the mountains **OR** on the beach?*

Would you rather...

*Receive a cute Valentine **OR** a funny one?*

Would you rather...

*Write a Valentine's Day poem **OR** make a Valentine's Day poster?*

Would you rather...

*Invent a new gadget **OR** discover a new scientific theory?*

Would you rather...

*Have smelly feet **OR** bad breath?*

Would you rather...

*Create a hand-made Valentine **OR** buy a pre-made one at the store?*

Would you rather...

*Read a book **OR** watch a movie of the book?*

Would you rather...

*Receive 100 roses **OR** 100 pieces of chocolate?*

Would you rather...

*Be Bruce Wayne **OR** Tony Stark?*

Would you rather...

*Give Valentines to all the boys in class **OR** all the girls?*

Would you rather...

*Live in space **OR** under the sea?*

Would you rather...

*Be completely alone **OR** have 100 people crammed into your house day on Valentine's Day?*

Would you rather...

*Clean the floor with a toothbrush **OR** mow the lawn with scissors?*

Would you rather...

*Get accidentally locked in the mall **OR** stuck at the airport on Valentine's Day?*

Would you rather...

*Have roses for fingers **OR** pieces of chocolate for eyes?*

Would you rather...

*Have the ability to fly **OR** read minds?*

Would you rather...

*Read a 2,000-page book about Valentine's Day **OR** write a 1,000-page book about it?*

Would you rather...

*Be a superhero **OR** a wizard?*

Would you rather...

*Have to write using red pen for the rest of your life **OR** dot all your "i"s and "j"s with hearts for the rest of your life?*

Would you rather...

*Do 100 pushups **OR** 100 situps?*

Would you rather...

*Be a famous actor **OR** a famous athlete?*

Would you rather...

*Shop for 2,000 gifts **OR** wrap 2,000 gifts?*

Would you rather...

*Get yelled at by Mom **OR** Dad?*

Would you rather...

*Only be awake at night **OR** during the day for Valentine's Day?*

Would you rather...

*Eat pizza for the rest of your life **OR** burgers?*

Would you rather...

*Get to direct a Valentine's Day special of your favorite TV show **OR** be the main actor/actress for the special?*

Would you rather...

Celebrate Valentine's Day every month **OR** *once every 10 years?*

Would you rather...

Have a runny nose **OR** *a stuffy nose?*

Would you rather...

*Never have to do homework again **OR** be paid to do your homework?*

Would you rather...

*Be really cold **OR** really hot?*

Would you rather...

*Sing a romantic song solo to an audience of 10 people **OR** wet your pants while receiving a Valentine?*

Would you rather...

*Lose your sense of touch **OR** smell?*

Would you rather...

*Light 1000 candles **OR** pick 1000 roses?*

Would you rather...

*Be super fast **OR** super strong?*

Would you rather...

*Have pink hair **OR** pink eyes?*

Would you rather...

*Never have to do homework again **OR** never take a test again?*

Would you rather...

*In front of the whole school, act out Romeo and Juliet **OR** sing your mom's favorite romantic song?*

Would you rather...

*Have a dinosaur **OR** a dragon as a pet?*

Would you rather...

Only be able to speak in love song lyrics **OR** only be able to speak in romantic movie quotes?

Would you rather...

Travel back in time **OR** to the future?

Would you rather...

Spend 2 days cooking a giant Valentine's Day meal **OR** 2 days cleaning up after the meal?

Would you rather...

Be really good at math **OR** writing?

Would you rather...

*Never eat chocolate **OR** never receive a Valentine?*

Would you rather...

*Always talk in riddles **OR** sing whenever you speak?*

Would you rather...

*Wear clown makeup for 6 months straight **OR** a pink tutu?*

Would you rather...

*On your first date, always have a booger showing in your nose **OR** food stuck in your teeth?*

Would you rather...

*Eat cookies **OR** cake?*

Would you rather...

*Be the most popular kid in school **OR** the smartest?*

Would you rather...

*Play inside all day **OR** outside?*

Would you rather...

*Be dressed up as Cupid **OR** Santa for a whole day?*

Would you rather...

*Live in Narnia **OR** in Hogwarts?*

Would you rather...

*Swim in a pool of red Jell-O **OR** red M&Ms?*

Would you rather...

*Eat healthy food and not exercise **OR** eat unhealthy food and exercise a lot?*

Would you rather...

*Have only 3 close friends **OR** many acquaintances?*

Would you rather...

Be forced to listen to music all the time **OR** *never listen to it?*

Would you rather...

Give one person a $1,000 gift **OR** *give 1,000 people a $1 gift?*

Would you rather...

Eat a Valentine's Day dinner covered in cranberry sauce **OR** gravy?

Would you rather...

Never have chocolate **OR** never watch a romantic movie?

Would you rather...

*Buy a pre-made house **OR** custom build one to your liking?*

Would you rather...

*Be a genius in a world of idiots **OR** an idiot in a world of geniuses?*

Would you rather...

Accidentally pee your pants in public **OR** *not brush your teeth for a week?*

Would you rather...

Be a teddy bear **OR** *a heart-shaped necklace?*

Would you rather...

Have your clothes be 2 sizes too small **OR** *2 sizes too big?*

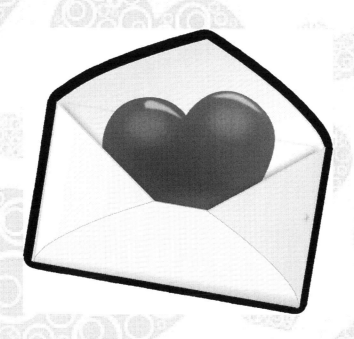

Would you rather...

Have to hug everyone you meet **OR** *give them a piece of chocolate?*

Enjoying the book so far?
Let us know what you think
by leaving a review!

What has been your
favorite question from the
book thus far?

Would you rather...

*Have two love birds sit on your shoulder for a week straight **OR** a big teddy bear follow you around?*

Would you rather...

*Spend a day with you favorite fictional character **OR** favorite celebrity?*

Would you rather...

*Eat rotten eggs **OR** drink rotten milk?*

Would you rather...

*Get many small Valentine's Day gifts **OR** one big one?*

Would you rather...

*Spend a day watching movies **OR** shopping at the mall?*

Would you rather...

*Receive socks **OR** a dictionary for Valentine's Day?*

Would you rather...

*Give up Valentine's Day **OR** St. Patrick's Day?*

Would you rather...

*Be able to read animal minds **OR** human minds?*

Would you rather...

*Dress up as Cupid for a week **OR** the Queen of Hearts?*

Would you rather...

*Spend a day with puppies **OR** kittens?*

Would you rather...

*Have a rock chip in your shoe **OR** a hair in your eye?*

Would you rather...

*Be gifted a Mercedes Benz **OR** a BMW?*

Would you rather...

*Have Cupid as your friend **OR** the Easter Bunny?*

Would you rather...

*Drive a Lamborghini **OR** Ferrari?*

Would you rather...

*Not celebrate your birthday **OR** Valentine's Day?*

Would you rather...

*Work at McDonald's **OR** Burger King?*

Would you rather...

*Have a third hand **OR** a third eye?*

Would you rather...

*Eat 2 pounds of candy in one sitting **OR** never be able to eat candy again?*

Would you rather...

*Get the best gift you ever received again **OR** take a chance on a new gift?*

Would you rather...

*Celebrate Christmas **OR** Halloween?*

Would you rather...

Spend Valentine's Day with your family **OR** with three celebrities of your choice?

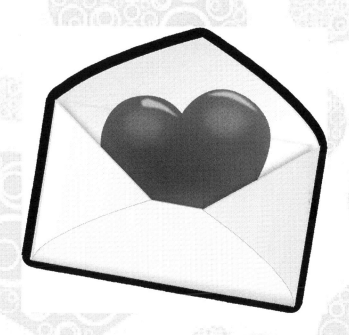

Would you rather...

Eat Indian food **OR** Mexican food?

Would you rather...

Get a papercut every time you touched paper **OR** bite your tongue every time you ate food?

Would you rather...

Be able to teleport **OR** read minds?

Would you rather...

*Wear your grandma's clothes **OR** have her hairstyle?*

Would you rather...

*Be famous for starring in a cheesy romantic movie **OR** not be famous at all?*

Would you rather...

*Lose the ability to lie **OR** believe everything you hear to be true?*

Would you rather...

*Hear the good news **OR** bad news first?*

Would you rather...

*Be the villain **OR** the hero in a movie?*

Would you rather...

*Have an arranged marriage **OR** never marry in your life?*

Would you rather...

*Be 4'0 **OR** 8'0?*

Would you rather...

*Be in constant pain **OR** have a constant itch?*

Would you rather...

*Give up your favorite pet **OR** never be able to use your cell phone?*

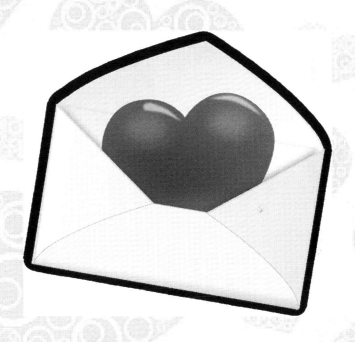

Would you rather...

*Use eyedrops made of lemon juice **OR** toilet paper made of sandpaper?*

Would you rather...

Take a guaranteed $100,000 **OR** take a 50/50 chance at $500,000?

Would you rather...

Never be able to take a hot shower again **OR** never eat hot food again?

Would you rather...

*Never play **OR** always play and never win?*

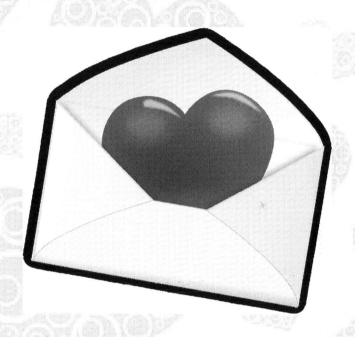

Would you rather...

*Know what all your gifts are **OR** be surprised by all your gifts?*

Would you rather...

*Be a chronic farter **OR** a chronic burper?*

Would you rather...

*Only have dessert on holidays **OR** never have dessert on holidays?*

Would you rather...

*Never use an electronic device ever again **OR** never talk to a human again?*

Would you rather...

*Be a vegetarian **OR** only be able to eat meat?*

Would you rather...

*Have 2 wishes today **OR** 3 wishes in 10 years?*

Would you rather...

*Go to a big party **OR** a small get together for Valentine's Day?*

Would you rather...

*Eat a stick of butter **OR** a teaspoon of cinnamon?*

Would you rather...

*Only be able to shout **OR** whisper everything you said?*

Would you rather...

*Have no Winter Break **OR** Spring Break?*

Would you rather...

*Be able to eat as much junk food as you want and not get fat **OR** receive a million dollars?*

Would you rather...

*Be able to see your own future **OR** other people's futures and not yours?*

Would you rather...

*Never remember faces **OR** names?*

Would you rather...

*Date the smartest **OR** cutest person in school?*

Would you rather...

*Receive a useful gift **OR** a fun gift?*

Would you rather...

*Star on a popular Valentine's Day music single **OR** in a popular Valentine's Day movie?*

Would you rather...

*Vacation somewhere cold **OR** hot during the holidays?*

Would you rather...

*Give up the internet for a month **OR** transportation?*

Would you rather...

*Spread love **OR** peace everywhere you go?*

Would you rather...

*Have your team mascot be Cupid **OR** a big piece of chocolate?*

Would you rather...

*Not be able to ask questions **OR** give answers?*

Would you rather...

*Have Cupid's wings **OR** his bow?*

Would you rather...

*Be rich and ugly **OR** poor and good looking?*

Would you rather...

*Receive a huge box of chocolates **OR** a huge teddy bear for Valentine's Day?*

Would you rather...

*Have all your presents wrapped terribly **OR** not wrapped at all?*

Thank you for reading! If you enjoyed the book, leave us a review and let us know what you liked or what you would like to see next.

As a special bonus, enjoy this exclusive preview of one our other popular titles!

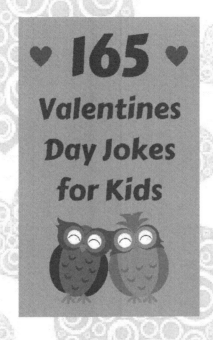

165

Valentines Day Jokes

For Kids

The Lovely Valentine's Day Gift

Book for Boys and Girls

Q: What did the bat say to his girlfriend?

A: I like hanging out with you.

Q: What happened when the man fell in love with his garden?

A: He wed (wet) his plants (pants)!

Q: Did you hear about the nearsighted porcupine?

A: He fell in love with a pincushion.

Q: What did the chocolate say to the ice cream?

A: You're real sweet!

Q: What did the paper clip say to the magnet?

A: I find you attractive.

Q: What did the French chef give his wife on Valentine's Day?

A: A hug and a quiche

Q: What did the ocean say to the chicken on Valentine's Day?

A: Nothing, it just waved.

Q: What did the squirrel say to her boyfriend on Valentine's Day?

A: You drive me so nuts!

Q: How did the telephone propose to his girlfriend?

A: He gave her a ring.

Q: What did the caveman give his girlfriend on Valentine's Day?

A: Lots of ughs and kisses!

Q: What did Steve say to his girlfriend? (Minecraft joke)

A: I dig you.

Q: What did the calculator say to the pencil on Valentine's Day?

A: You can count on me!

Q: What did the bee say to his girlfriend on Valentine's Day?

A: You are bee-utiful!

Q: What did the sheep say to her boyfriend on Valentine's Day?

A: You're not too baaaa-d.

Q: What did Frankenstein say to his Valentine?

A: Will you be my Valenstein?

Q: What happened to the two angels that got married?

A: They lived harpily ever after!

Q: What's the most romantic city in the UK?

A: Loverpool

Q: What did the raspberry say to the strawberry on Valentine's Day?

A: I love you berry much!

If you enjoyed this title,

check out our other books

by searching "Hayden Fox"

on Amazon!

Manufactured by Amazon.ca
Bolton, ON

11059152R00052